D1453537

ACTIVE LISTENING 2.0

Overcoming Stalls and Objections by Asking the Right Questions at the Right Time

STEVE TRANG

JONES MEDIA
PUBLISHING

Printed in the United States of America

ISBN: 978-1-948382-10-6 paperback
JMP2020.1

CONTENTS

CHAPTER 1

Introduction to Active Listening

Active listening is one of the most important skills needed to succeed in the twenty-first century. Unfortunately, it is still not a commonly understood term. As a result, many people are still unable to adopt it in their daily lives. The truth is that you can get more out of life by learning how to listen actively. Let's take a moment to explore active listening.

Active listening is a technique that is used in different areas of life such as counselling, conflict resolution, and training. Active listening involves the listener paying full attention to what the speaker is saying. The listener should also be able to respond, remember what was said, and understand it fully.

This listening technique is different from *reflective listening* and *emphatic listening.* Neither technique places an emphasis on understanding the words of the speaker. Your active-listening skill will influence the quality of your communication with others. Active listening can benefit you with its numerous applications, such as in journalism, tutoring, counselling suicidal people, interactions between medical practitioners and patients, HIV counselling, and so on. The importance of this listening technique has also been identified to be an effective tool in sales, which is what we'll be taking a look at in this book.

Active Listening 2.0 goes beyond to just listening. 2.0 requires a salesperson to become skillful enough to extract the meaning and intent behind every question and statement shared by the prospect. By asking the right questions at the right time, the prospect will willingly share what's on their mind and the keys to providing the solutions they want.

How can you adopt active listening to become a better salesperson? Did you know that the proper use of active listening can get people to open up and let you know what they really want? Just imagine the benefits that you would enjoy from this. With your improved communication skills, you would know the right questions to ask and when to ask them.

What Is the Importance of a Selling Framework?

Almost everything about human life relates to sales. Many people view sales as just the exchange of goods/services for money, but it's much more than that. A lot of processes describe any sale. Amateurish sales personnel would try to approach each individual sale head-on. However, a selling framework describes the complex phases that salespeople have to be pass through before successful selling can occur. Yes, the selling framework is a repeatable process which is formed based on customer buying behavior.

With a framework in place, you and your salespeople know what to do at every stage of the selling process.

In recent times, most businesses are advised to adopt a framework. The framework is usually adopted based on the prospects of such a sale. There are numerous business structures out there with some as old as humankind. You may have heard that the oldest business in the world is prostitution, but I would argue that prostitution only became a business once somebody was able to <u>sell</u> the services.

Selling has been around for as long as we can remember. Because sales has been around so long, we intuitively know when we're being sold to, and as a result, we've created a counter-sales strategy without even knowing it.

That is why we naturally always keep our cards close to the chest when we talk to a salesperson. Why else would we say the clichéd "I'm just looking" any time we walk into a store? We walked into the store to buy something. Shouldn't we ask the professional for help?

This reminds me of my experience watching TV shows. I found it quite difficult to watch TV shows because I felt they were stereotypes. In fact, ever since I got cable, I can recollect only watching a few shows. In my opinion, they felt misleading and seemed like they would do anything just to buy more time and keep you glued to the screen. I realized this was the wrong way to get people to watch your show. Eventually, I managed to find a few ones that kept my attention: *South Park* and *House*.

I found Dr. House especially useful because of how they handled the show. They chose to be different from others. It was a medical show, but not the usual ones you see around. The doctor on the show understood that everybody lies, especially when you are in a buyer-seller relationship with them. To deal with the lies and be able to accurately diagnose the patient, the doctor chose to look beyond the lies of the patient.

Dr. House had other doctors that worked for him. These doctors had a simple job: get into the house of the patient and record whatever information you can find. This information would describe the lives of the patient before they got sick and was vital to the diagnosis, helping them treat people better. This show highlights a unique way of handling a selling framework. They chose to eliminate the lies and focus on what really matters for the best service delivery. You have to emulate this type of problem-solving for your own business.

Get familiar with some things you are likely to hear from customers and develop responses to them. This is what the selling framework is concerned with. As the owner of a brand, you should know how best to settle the common requests and lies that the buyer may throw your way. This framework will give you a solid structure and prevent you from having to start from scratch every time that you come across a new customer.

There may be times when the customers are only trying to make inquiries about a product but not yet interested in making a purchase. This type of customer may try to disguise their inquiry like an actual desire to purchase. You should be able to identify these types of scenarios and change the situation of things to suit your motives:

making a sale. The selling framework is going to contain information about this.

Think about it. What would they say? Then, what would be your reply? There is no doubt that there are a variety of ways in which a scenario could turn out. But you can't also deny the fact that there are questions and statements that you hear often. Customers or clients invariably have similar requests, and this makes the selling framework a repeatable process because you can do it again and again.

The way you handle a customer's inquiries and buying behavior will go a long way to determine your overall conversions. Due to this, you need to become better at active listening. The listening techniques will ensure that you understand the customer's demands, remember them, and provide effective solutions to them.

By establishing the selling framework, you have set the ground rules for how to handle sales. The rules for anything are an important element of life. Don't shy away from marking the boundaries for the framework and deciding on a course of action to guide your activities. When meetings are arranged, an outline of activities is written to guide the activities of the meeting. It is this same way that you would draw an outline to serve as your selling framework.

Customers will tell you many things, and you have to be able to understand clearly what they mean to determine your best course of action. Active listening will help you take advantage of the opportunities that come your way with targeted questions.

CHAPTER 2

Uncover Meaning and Intent

If you are in sales, you might think that you'll need to talk a lot. It's important that you know how to control or drive conversations. Some customers often mistake this as the salesperson trying to do so much to sell. The prospects may feel like they are being pushed. It's important to communicate differently. You need to understand that it is not about what you say. It's not even how you say it. It's how the prospect receives and processes your message that ultimately matters.

Why is "how you say it" important? Well, you need to know that regardless of what you say, the interpretation of the buyer is what will determine their action. If they like what they hear, they will proceed to the next stage of the selling process, and if they don't, they'll take their business elsewhere. At the end of the day, it doesn't matter what your intent is; the most important thing is how the prospect perceives it.

The problem is that we're dealing with very old hardware. As a species, we're only slightly better than our cavemen ancestors. While our brain is operating like a computer, our ability to communicate is only about as good as dial-up internet. The tool we have to talk and listen to one another would be comparable to handing somebody a spoon and asking them to build a pool in their backyard. Recent studies have suggested that our brains operate at twenty million bits per second, while our language can handle seven bits per second.

The truth is that you can pass a message in a variety of words, using different combinations of words, and the listener would still interpret it differently. It's just not about what you say to the prospect but how you say it and how they come to understand it. Have you ever wondered why when talking to certain people, they never seem to understand you regardless of what you say? The problem here is not what you are saying but how you said it. You may not say anything wrong and the message will completely be perceived as that.

To explain this better, let's take a look at a certain scenario. Ever since I was twenty-one, I had visited the casino every Friday afternoon. After some time, everyone became aware of this fact—when I arrived a few hours late, it was quite noticeable. I am now married with kids, so those days are over. Let's pretend my friends want me to go play some poker with them. I immediately agree with my friends without seeking consent from my wife and only ask her, "Hey dear, I'm going to the casino with the boys. Can you watch the kids?" Now, it may seem like I have said something completely harmless, but it may lead to an argument if my wife finds my message unappealing.

However, if I go about asking her about whether we have plans for the night, then my wife's perception of my request will be different. This theory applies to everything in life. We have been conditioned to ask questions the wrong way for a long time.

We need to re-learn how to ask questions the right way. When we review our lives, we understand that we have been asking questions the wrong way for quite some time now.

Asking Questions the Right Way and How That Influences Sales

When asking questions or dealing with people, it's important to note that you are oblivious to whatever is going on in the other person's world. You may think you know or want to assume things, but that won't work out well for you in your business in the long run. It's safe not to assume anything about the prospect's world and try to find out vital information from ground zero.

How does this relate to sales? You must be able to find out the mind of the prospect without assuming too much. The mind of the prospect is an individual entity and will always act on its own free will. A homeowner wants to sell his property and has the option of dealing with two investors, A and B. Investor A is the first to come into the scene and offers a massive payout but requires the homeowner to close the property in seven days. Investor A hopes to secure the deal by offering a lucrative money offer, assuming that is what the prospect will find most appealing. Investor B adopts a different approach and decides on what will make the client happier. Investor B offers less money but offers the prospect the chance of staying in the property for two extra months. To Investor A's surprise, the homeowner decided to sell to Investor B simply because he agreed more with the overall offer he got. The payout was NOT the deciding factor.

In the world of sales, you may think that you have a perfect idea of what the customer's demands are, but this will only lead to errors. You must find out exactly what the needs of each customer are and how to tackle them. Investor A in the example above could have approached the whole scenario differently and gotten better results than he did with his first trial. First of all, he shouldn't have set a short and compulsory timeline for the prospect. Many people feel choked when they have to strictly follow certain timelines or regulations to complete a sale. Investor A could have expressed his desire to close the sale within the next seven days, but instead of assuming that his offer was favorable, he could have asked the prospect for what would have been a favorable timeframe to close the sale or exit the house. By doing this, you relinquish some aspects of control back to the prospect and they are free to make their decision actively. When a client feels like you are exerting too much control over the deal, they will back out more often than not. Listen to the clients, know what they want, and create your proposal around that. By doing this, they will find it harder to turn you down.

Asking Better Questions

As someone in sales, you need to know how to balance the conversation. Just like the scenario discussed above, you can't do all the talking. If you do most of the talking, then you will end up losing too many sales. As a seller, you should avoid rambling on and on about how great your product is and why the prospect should patronize you. When you talk too much, you begin to sound desperate and the prospect will begin to wonder if you are being entirely truthful. Give the prospect a chance to speak freely and voice their concerns. You just may be able to learn more about them from what they say. If you do most of the talking here, you will most likely never get the sale.

There may be certain prospects who will continuously ask you questions about yourself. Now, are they interested in your story or your personality? No. Then, why are they asking questions about my experience in the business? Well, they are only trying to find out if you are really who you say you are and determining how much you can perform. When answering questions from prospects, you must learn how to give out only vital information. Find out what they want to hear. Why are they asking you that question? Could I help their decision about the sale? Don't answer cluelessly and end up rambling about a thing the client doesn't want to hear.

When they ask you a question, you must be clear on what their intentions are. If you are unsure, you can immediately ask a direct question for clarification. This will save you a lot of headaches and help you give the best answer that could close the sale. Just like it was clearly stated earlier that you know nothing about their world and where they are coming from, it would be a good tactic to just play dumb here. Let them show you the way and lead you to what they want. The best way to let them lead is by relinquishing control and taking your time to listen and digest what they are saying, as if you don't know anything.

There is also another common mistake which many salespeople make when dealing with their prospects. As soon as the salesperson has gained a reasonable amount of knowledge about the job from past experience they stop listening. There are some times when it may feel like you know the answer to the question even before it was asked. This could tempt the salesperson to give preemptive answers that may irk the prospect. When you begin to answer questions before they are finished asking, the prospects will feel like they are not being listened to. Yes, you may have answered the question correctly, but they would feel rushed and dissatisfied. Even if you are sure about what their question will be, let them finish asking before offering up an answer. In some cases, you may even go ahead to demand extra clarification before letting them hear what they would want to hear.

You will realize that you will become a better salesperson when you stop acting like you know the answers to all the questions. Learn to hold back a little and make it seem like you are barely coming to terms with what is being discussed. Yes, be confident in answering questions but don't be cocky! Even when the prospect is asking you a ridiculously simple question, you want to give him faith that you are the right person for the job without sounding too exertive. Make it seem like you are trying to work with him to reach a reasonable solution. They tend to appreciate this more. They will feel like a part of the process, reveal more about themselves, and work with you to achieve a reasonable solution.

The moment you stop acting like you know the solution to everything, then things will get better. This is certainly a different approach from what you are used to, but it works! Just understand that the sale is a process and you just have to get it right.

Another important rule to note on communicating effectively with your prospects is that you should never give answers to questions that were never asked.

This may be hard to do, but try to take statements for just what they are: mere statements. If a question is asked, come up with a suitable approach and answer the question.

For instance, take a look at this typical conversation between a prospect and salesperson:

Prospect: "We like your presentation. Your price is really high." When most salespeople hear this, they might be quick to drop their price and go for the close. This is a statement that needs to be investigated further. You could respond with, "Our price is high?" or "What were you expecting our bid to come in at?" The desire to become defensive or pounce will kill a lot of sales.

Watch out for statements that sound like objections. The prospect may say things like: "We are looking at other options," "We asked some relatives for help on this," "My younger sister is a Realtor," " Your offer is too low," and so on. These are statements, and you don't have to respond to them. In fact, never answer them unless the prospect requests an answer from you. The reason behind this is because these statements are thoughts of the prospect which are merely expressed during their conversations with you. Now, these thoughts do not mean they will accept or decline your offer. However, they mean that the client is thinking about your offer. This means you have caught their attention and that is a great thing to accomplish. Now, where the sale would proceed from here depends on how you handle the entire process. But now, you have been able to identify the interest of the customer in your offer.

Lost Puppy

There's another stage we affectionately refer to as "Lost Puppy." Imagine if this morning, as you're walking out getting ready to go to the office, you open the door, and there's a little puppy right outside your front door. Ninety percent of you will pick up that puppy. You would just love that puppy and try to rescue that puppy.

We're doing the same exact thing here in our appointments. We want the prospects to feel good about themselves, so we want to come across as needing help. I'll give you a couple examples here: one of my first jobs was as a server. And being a server on my first day, I got better tips than any other days. Why? Because I was awful. I was horrendous. It was very clear that I was nervous. I could barely handle the tray. (And by the way, I'm really impressed with some of the servers and everything they can hold because my holding just a few glasses was always a challenge.) Anyhow, I got some massive tips. The reason why I got such good tips is because a handful of people felt really bad for me. They thought, "If we don't give this kid some larger tips, this kid might go hungry."

Same thing in real estate. When I first started as a real estate agent. Someone asked me a question. I wrote all the questions down and asked, "Did I get that question, right? Okay, great. Let me call my broker, and then I'll give you the answer." I would call them back. "Talked to my broker. Here's what we said . . ." and they'll be happy.

I got experienced, stopped writing down the questions, and stopped having to ask my broker, because I'd have the answer. I reached a point then where it got so routine that I knew the answer before they even finish asking the question. Of course, I wasn't so rude to finish their question for them, but what happened? I went from this guy that was borderline competent to this guy that's a slick professional. Once I became the slick professional and had the answer for everything, prospects started thinking, "Can I really trust this guy?"

I started having success again once I stopped assuming that I had all the answers. I started asking more questions and genuinely tried to understand exactly the motivations behind the prospect's concerns. I was no longer this overconfident salesperson. I became a trusted advisor.

Have you ever had a situation where you were asking a question, and someone cut you off, giving you an answer that had nothing to do with your question? Or you cut off someone else's question, and they were totally frustrated? Even if you had the right answer, the fact that you cut them off will cause them to feel unheard or unappreciated.

Here is something that happened with me and my brokerage. We get served sometimes for wage garnishment. Periodically, one of our agents will receive a judgment for wage garnishment. If they were a W2 employee, that means that I would have to take funds out of their wages to pay down the judgment. Because I'm a brokerage and all the agents are 1099 independent contractors, they're not employees, and I can't garnish their wages. When we get wage garnishment notices, we file them and do nothing with them.

One day, I get an angry phone call from an attorney. And she says, "You haven't responded to our wage garnishment notice." I apologized. Told her that my attorney said that we don't need to respond to them because real estate agents are independent contractors. She became angry, and said, "No, you have to respond to these. This is a problem." I responded, "Well, can you just let me know which code or whatever it is we got wrong. I will go talk to my attorney, tell him what we did wrong. Please send me an email about what we did wrong. I'll be sure to let him know. And we'll respond."

She's very frustrated now, and instructs, "No, I'm not your attorney." I asked, "What am I supposed to tell him? I don't even know what to tell him. If you can just tell me what to tell him." She snapped, "I'm not your attorney!" Getting into lost puppy mode, I responded sheepishly, "Boy, I'm so sorry. I didn't get a chance to go to law school. I'm just a real estate agent. I don't know what is going on here." Feeling bad for me, she said, "Okay, fine. What's your email?" She then emailed me what I needed!

Playing Hard to Get

Let's go back to high school or college. If you remember, the bad boy always got the girls. The good boys don't get them. Why? Because the bad boys don't care, right? They're playing it really cool. Likewise, that girl that everyone was after that was irresistible was always playing hard to get.

That's our mindset and mantra. We push a lot of people away by assuming the best-case scenario or telling the prospects how they don't need us. Here are some examples of this:

I don't know . . .

I don't suppose . . .

I'm not sure . . .

When prospects ask us if we can help them, our answers generally start with one of those three statements. It sounds odd. Seems like we should have all the answers. Remember, this one simple fact, though: You are an expert in your industry, but you don't know their situation. You're not sure of your prospect's budget, timeframe, or decision-making process. For that reason, you don't really know if you can help them yet. And by being unsure, you're gaining permission to ask questions.

We always want to be pulling away because if we're pulling away, they're going to pull us in. As opposed to most salespeople that are being pushy with massive commission breath. The last time you ran into a pushy salesperson, did you enjoy it? Or did you repel them? Exactly.

The natural action is if we're pushing, they're going to pull. If we pull, they may let us pull away, which is great! Now we're saving time because we know that the prospect wasn't that serious. However, if they fight back by saying, "No, no, no. I need you," and they try to reach out and grab you, now you're in a really good spot.

Caution! You really need to watch your tone. You can come across as a sarcastic jerk if you say it with the wrong tone. Practice with your peers, and be careful!

To get the most information, you'll want to ask *What* and *How* questions. *Who* and *When* questions generally lead to very short answers that may be entirely unhelpful. Additionally, prospects can easily give false or misleading answers. *Why* questions can come across accusatory in nature, even if you are being genuinely curious. Remember, our goal is to come across as a trusted adviser or consultant. Asking questions like "Who are the decision makers?" and "When will you make a decision?" causes you to start sounding like a salesperson. It will kill a lot of the rapport and trust that you build up until this point.

My two favorite questions are "What happens next?" and "How will you know you're working with the right person?" Do you see how powerful they are? The prospects will tell you what you need to do to win their business!

My two daughters had a piano recital where I was one of the parent volunteers. It was me and another parent, who was also a school teacher. She has experience dealing with rowdy kids. We're standing outside the recital hall while the other kids are playing and performing. The kids we're watching are getting kind of loud and rambunctious. She says to the kids, "Hey, I have an idea. Let's play a game. I'm thinking of a number between one and one hundred."

One of the kids asked, "Is it more or less than fifty?" That's the question that 90 percent of us are going to ask. My daughter asks, "What's the tens digit?" Being a proud father, I thought "Hey, that's a great question!" Immediately we go from a hundred possibilities to ten. After asking what's the single digit, you've got the number. The only better question is, "What's the number?"

Unfortunately, when she asked, "What's the tens digit?" the parent helper responded with, "You can't ask that question. That's against the rules." Remember the earlier section about proper communication? Why is this question against the rules? What lesson did my daughter learn here? How to not ask good questions. That was my takeaway from witnessing this.

Stop asking yes-no questions. This is a filthy habit. I'm still guilty of this one from time to time. This happens often by ending your great questions with the following terms: Right? Correct? Agree? Doesn't it? Wouldn't it?

For example, "It sounds like you're pretty frustrated" would turn into "You're pretty frustrated, right?" You turned a great statement designed to uncover information from a prospect to a one-word answer.

Remember, we want them to volunteer information.

When you're asking yes-no questions, you are giving the prospect the telemarketer experience. Telemarketers have been taught that if the prospect says yes to enough questions, they will say yes when asked to buy. Do you like water? Yes. Do you like water that tastes clean? Yes. Well, then you should check out our water purification system. That's not the experience we're going for. We're shooting for open-ended questions, not yes-no questions.

Another powerful tool is awkward silence. You just pause, and you just wait. Just count beats. If you get to a point when you feel uncomfortable, you can break the silence by stating, "Share what's on your mind." Awkward silence is uncomfortable. Your counterpart will fill in that vacuum because that's better than the alternative . . . being uncomfortable.

Are you sending a lot of brochures? We used to. What a waste of paper, envelopes, and stamps. When prospects asked us to send them information, we couldn't wait!

Yes, let me send you information so that you might like it and buy from me. We don't do that anymore. No more sending brochures, website info, or emailing documents. The only time we will send anything is if we know for sure something positive is going to happen. How will we know? We ask!

"Let's pretend I send you the brochure, and you take the time to review it. If you like what you see, what happens next?" If the next words out of their mouths isn't about us doing business together, then we're not sending anything. If they say they don't know or they'll need to talk to some other person, don't waste your time or resources. I kick myself over how much time and money I wasted over the years sending marketing pieces.

Sometimes, you'll understand the pain that your prospect is going through. The problem is, they won't have any idea that you can empathize with their pain. There is one simple way to demonstrate that, though. You just need to acknowledge it! Make sure you're not just feeling their pain. Acknowledge their pain verbally. When you're dealing with an adult that's going through pain, and you acknowledge it, we're doing the adult version of addressing their boo-boo.

When you watch a kid in the playground, and they fall down and scrape their knee, mom comes over, touches it, kisses it, kid smiles, and they're on their way. Same phenomenon is occurring here. This is just the adult version of addressing their boo-boo. By acknowledging, you're immediately conveying that you're listening. You'll want to make sure you apply a lot of assumptive statements:

Sounds like you're frustrated.

Seems like you're getting a lot of phone calls.

Feels like it's over.

Feels like you're frustrated.

By acknowledging, you're reducing the power. Again, just for emphasis, pause. Let your acknowledgement marinate.

A funny thing happens when you make assumptive statements. When you're right, you win; when you're wrong, your prospect will happily tell you!

Just think about when you're in a Facebook forum or Facebook group or on YouTube or Reddit, or any other website, and someone asks a question. People might answer. They might not. However, when a person gets angry, and they make a strong statement. People are going to jump in and correct that person.

What happens here is that we're too busy. We're all really too busy to answer someone's question. But when someone makes a statement that you disagree with, oh, you've got time to correct them. We all have time to put people in their places. Especially now with our crazy polarized environment. And if you make an assumptive statement that's wrong, people are happy to correct it.

I'll give an example of where this happened (I did this on accident; I didn't know what I was doing). I was talking to my buddy, Brandon, and he was having a gender reveal party. Not one of those where we burn down the entire forest. This was just something private at his home. He called me on a Wednesday, "Hey, Steve, are you coming on Friday night?" I jokingly responded, "Brandon, I don't need to come to the gender reveal party. I already know, you're having a boy."

He blurts out, "No, we're having a girl." What happened? I made a statement, and he corrected it. If I said, "Brandon, I'm really busy. I'm kind of tired," and ask if he's having a boy or girl, he's going to be ready for that. Okay, so by assuming poorly, we'll get the correct answer. I would guess 99 percent of the population are not going to lie through a correction. And people love to correct. They can't get enough of it. As a result, it's the best way to make progress in a conversation.

CHAPTER 3

Establish Rules

Many salespeople underestimate the importance of setting ground rules for the sales network. At this stage, you should already have been putting some rules into place and making sure that everyone one on your team follows the rules to the letter. These rules are set to determine the engagement between seller and prospect during their first and subsequent meetings. These will be the rules that will guide the activities between both parties. Just like the rules of your favorite sport have been set in stone, you should prepare the rules of engagement before going forward with anything.

Think about it. What are the important elements of your meeting? The first important thing to note is the purpose of the meeting. Ask yourself: Why are you here? What's the point of the meeting between both parties? What is the expected outcome? Take a look at the agenda of your prospect. Do they agree with yours? Take note of similar points of interest. They will make up the purpose of your meeting.

If you fail to determine the agenda of the meeting, both parties may end up wasting time on trivialities that do not contribute to overall success. After you have established the ground rules for your meetings, make sure to introduce it to your prospect as soon as they express their interest to deal with you. By making them aware of the ground rules, the client will always be aware of what is going on and will feel part of the entire process. Make it clear to them that this is how such meetings usually go and that you are only following set protocols.

Ask for their permission before you go ahead to state the purpose of the meeting to avoid looking suspicious to them. If you just begin to state your rules, they may feel insecure and scared of your true intentions. Tailor your speech to suit the setting of the meeting: either physical or virtual. The purpose of the meeting should make you feel like you are invited and relinquish control over the affairs to them. Don't forget the lessons discussed in the last chapter about your speech and approach to the prospect. Never impose yourself on the meeting or conversation. Instead, let your tone and words indicate that you are ready to listen to their demands.

The perfect duration for a meeting is an hour or an hour and a half. Inform them of the required duration for the meeting and find out what they think. If they do not have enough time on their hands for the meeting, it's time to reschedule. The reason behind this is that a short duration will make you rush and the meeting will fail to get into any flow. Basically, they will only pay attention to the price of your offer and nothing else.

It's important not to pressure your prospects—give them enough time to grasp all details and come to a decision. Break down complex aspects of the process into bits and simplify it. You would want to make everything as simple, reasonable and understandable as possible. Ensure that all the terms and vocabulary that you will use are simple enough for a third-grader to understand. When this has been achieved, you can say that your marketing was effective.

Most prospects will only be concerned about how much the sale would cost and how they can get it to enjoy the product or service. Do your best to be clear about this aspect because it can make or break the whole sale.

As the meeting progresses, the prospect will begin to ask you questions. Yes, you may be intelligent enough to remember the questions but you can do better: write them down. By writing the questions, it indicates that you are actually listening and noting key points of the prospect. The points you note down can help you a lot as you go on with the conversation.

Take note that before you ask personal questions you would need to ask permission. It's important to ask for permission to make sure it doesn't appear like you are peering into their privacy. When asking a personal question, ensure you are direct and get straight to the point, or it's likely your motives get questioned. Let them also understand why you are asking details about their personal lives. Many prospects think everything is just about buying and selling and find it hard to understand the need to give out personal info. The type of merchandise or service you are selling will determine the type of questions you will throw at prospects.

There was a time when I would ask my prospects some of these personal questions without necessarily asking for their permission. Yes, some people would answer just to make sure they get things done. However, there is always this awkwardness in the air that is hard to shake off. You would save yourself from lots of hassle by going through everything step-by-step. There may even be some people who may begin to question you when you start to pry into their personal affairs. If you asked for permission earlier, all you need to do is remind them of the agreement. When dealing with people who refuse to divulge personal information, don't push them or try to coerce them. As soon as you have identified that they don't want to reveal the vital information you are asking, you can politely leave.

At the end of the meeting, one of two things is possible. It's either the sale is successful or not. Whichever way it goes, there's no need to panic. If you have done your best, then the sale was likely not to happen. Remember that you are a stranger in the prospect's world and just have to accept their decisions. That's why it's important to direct the conversation to where you want it using your selling framework.

The whole conversation shouldn't just be about them. You can share something about you, such as your biggest fear. Your biggest fear should speak about the challenges or difficulties that you have faced when working with previous prospects before them.

CHAPTER 4

Uncover Pain and Motivation

Considering my experience in sales, there is always a lot of talk about pain and being able to find pain or identify it. Now, the kind of pain which we are talking about here isn't physical but experienced pain.

When you are able to identify their pain and how they feel about it, you can also identify their limitations and how far they are willing to go with the sale. Buying decisions is an emotional process. For many people, they buy first before thinking about the consequences. This could end up hurting them when they realize that they don't need their latest purchase as much as they thought they would. After these people have suffered lots of pain from making poor purchase choices, they find it hard to make up their mind on future decisions. They are simply just too scared to take a leap of faith forward and make the purchase. They fear a reoccurrence of whatever caused them regret in the past.

Let's take a look at an example. I love cars, and I always try to have a fun car to drive. When I was much younger, I bought an Audi S4. I managed to get it at a much cheaper price. Retail sold the car at about $68,000–$80,000, while I got a used Audi of the same model at $35,000. I was elated and it sounded like the best deal of the year for me. When I bought the car, it had been used for three years and had a mileage count of just over 35,000 miles. The car handled well and took corners smoothly. It was a time of bliss for me as long as the car stayed under the extended warranty. When the mileage count hit about 61,000, I could feel the car slowly start to come apart and things weren't running well. As soon as the warranty expired, I would take the car in and had to make repairs. This process is known as planned obsolescence.

I would go into the dealership for repairs and sit in the cars on the showroom floors. As I sat in the car, I would smell the new car smell. Feel the stitching in the leather steering wheel and the bucket seats welcomed me, picturing myself in the latest model of the car. And of course, I get to thinking: You know, my payment on my current car is $328/mo. I just spent $3000 on repairs. Broken into twelve months, that's $250/mo. Add them together, and I can justify spending $578/mo.

And it wasn't before long, I got into a brand-new car at exactly $578/mo. And this is the classic example of buying emotionally and justifying intellectually. It was a very bad financial decision, but I enjoyed that car for a few years!

Have a look at another example of an emotional buying decision. I liked the Tesla Model X and wanted to get it for my family, but my wife just wasn't interested in driving something like that. She felt the car was almost as expensive as a house and wasn't necessary at that point. In order to convince her, I let her in on some facts, such as the car was presently the safest to drive when compared to other options.

I also argued that what makes a house a home is the people in it. So wouldn't it make sense to spend as much on a car to protect the people that make a house a home? She understood my point and the car was purchased. Now, I am not saying that this decision was free of its financial drawbacks. However, we had justified the reason for purchasing the car, and regardless of what happened, the car would serve its purpose and give us satisfaction.

As a salesperson, your job is to look out for opportunities without getting attached. If you walk into McDonald's to get a Big Mac and the cashier asks if you would want fries or coke, what do you think is happening here? Is she trying to convince you? Definitely not. If you decide not to get what she has offered you, she won't feel bad about it and she'll move on to serving the next customer. This is the same attitude you should have toward your job. Your job is to find people that either want to sell or buy from you. It's an exchange, and you definitely don't need to waste hours convincing anyone. Your work should speak for you.

Not everyone you come across in your line of business is "the customer." Some are just there to make inquiries. Learn to detach yourself emotionally from your sales or you risk suffering some pain when things don't go how you want them. Yes, you should want to close as many sales as possible, but you just can't sell to everyone you find.

When talking to prospects, you have to be prepared to handle people that will get emotional. Just like me, you may not feel very comfortable handling emotional people, but you definitely have no choice. People like this could spend long durations going on and on about different things without addressing the matter at hand. Such people could have problems at home, someone depending on them, problems at work, and other pressing issues. Due to this, they can easily get carried away when trying to make decisions on sales. As soon as you have noticed this type of prospect who is failing to focus on the subject matter, you can gently call back their attention to the matter at hand and try to positively control their attention. Don't be hard on them or shrug them off. They are people too, and their current predicaments don't mean you can't still get a sale over the line. It's just important that you handle them by paying attention to details. Listen to everything they say and encourage them when it seems like their emotions are starting to build up. This is an important point to note. You won't have to deal with this type of customer every time, but it's worth knowing what to do in such situations.

There is a way to control a conversation without making the prospect feel pressured or in a tight corner. To explain this further, I would like to narrate an encounter which I had at the doctor's office. This encounter actually gives a lot of insight into the image I am trying to paint.

Have you ever wondered why doctors never attend to you on time and why you have to do so much just to get some time with them? I think there may be some kind of training that doctors get that makes them collude to waste as much of everybody's time as possible. I showed up at the doctor's office by 8:00 a.m. as always. I am already feeling irritated because I know that I will have to wait for some time for the doctor. I went in to get the insurance card even though it has not changed for the last few years. After a little argument with administration, I was sent to the scale to have my weight taken and they run some tests on me, mostly blood work. Then, I still have to wait for a few minutes before I get to see the doctor. Finally, after having lost an hour, I'm in the doctor's office. The doctor starts with some small talk. I've been waiting all morning, losing valuable time to work. Small talk is the last thing I need right now. Let's just get straight to the point and move on.

Now he's going through my medical records and the results of my last blood work. And he's saying, "This is good. This is good. This is good." And he looks at one thing and pauses. He immediately gets my attention. In my mind, I am wondering what is going on. He breaks the silence and asks, "Steve, does anyone in your family have a history of liver disease?"

My mind is all over the place because I have no clue what is going on. Liver disease? I don't know what I answered as my mind was still all over the place. Right now, I am doing my best to keep my emotions in check. Then the doctor continues by saying I possibly have liver problems. According to him, it could either be a tumor in the liver, hepatitis, or I'm just overweight. At this point, the only thing on my mind was survival. I just had my third child, and I was ready to pay anything to make sure that I was okay. Money was no object to me right then.

Little did I know that he was simply trying to upsell me, because he got me to do the ultrasound. I even called my assistant and told her to cancel all my previous appointments. That was how serious it sounded. Voila! The test results came back negative: it turns out that I was just overweight. Since then I have been working out and lost considerable weight.

How did the doctor do that to me? Well, you have to learn how to control the conversation like that and keep the prospect engaged. This is the same thing that we see lawyers do all the time on TV shows. In court, a lawyer would never ask a question they don't know the answer to. Also, each question is meant to make a point and lead to a certain point. Yes, you have to learn how to do this. Don't ask questions in areas that you aren't good with and have no business knowing about. By being direct and decisive, you keep the attention of the prospect on what you are saying.

When you get into the doctor's office, they don't just go ahead and hand over pills, as most of us would like. They make us sit and begin to ask questions they probably already knew the answer to. When they are done with their observation, the meeting will end. Doctors or lawyers will ask questions without caring what your immediate reaction or emotional state will be. They know they are just doing their job. You must learn that type of control. Be nice and confident but detach yourself from your personal emotions or feelings of the sale. Try to take them a few months back in their life or identify a point in their lives that could support your sale. Perhaps, there is an underlying need which you are unaware of.

So, the prospect wants to buy your product because X is causing them to feel the way they are feeling. How can they deal with X? Present your product as the solution.

You can ask them to tell you if they are ready to deal with the problem—not necessarily through you.

Make sure you noted everything discussed in this chapter. The established rules are more important than you think. First impressions can last for a very long time. It's vital that you get the first meeting right. Like I said earlier, getting the deal done here shouldn't be your goal; getting the prospect's commitment is why you are doing all this. They have to be able to trust you enough to do business with you. As soon as you have gotten the prospect to trust you, only three things can prevent the deal from being done: money, timing, and other people. It's important to ask which of these would be the problem and get all objections out of the way.

CHAPTER 5

Uncover Price

I like to refer to the stage of uncovering price as the Money Dance. This is actually because both parties will go back and forth on negotiations in almost like a dance pattern. It is during this phase that you have to identify the quality that the customer is looking forward to, how much the deal could cost either party, and so on. This will be anything but straightforward.

When you have gotten the commitment of the customer as in the previous chapter, only either of three things can make the sale fall through: price, timing, and other people. This stage is usually the most difficult for most sales professionals. However, you are about to learn how to conquer the stage and engage the prospect. How do you get to agree on a price? There are quite a few things I like to do here.

The first thing you can try is the family approach. According to my experience, customers discuss the elements of an upcoming sale/purchase with family members or close friends when they are interested in it. They just can't help it. You can say something like: "History has shown to me that people talk to family members or close friends about an impending sale. Did you discuss an acceptable price would them? Would you mind sharing with me what it is so that we can work something out?" By saying these things you affirm to your prospect that

- you've been doing this for quite some time,

- you rely on your experience,

- they can trust you with information.

Remember what we said about communication and watching how you say a thing more than what you say. This way, they easily share what you want to hear. If after you have asked and they still don't seem like they would budge, don't push them. Change the subject matter and continue the conversation. The product that you are offering for sale obviously has a price, but there are times when the customer would prefer that you are flexible with them.

You can give them a price range based on your competition. This will help you figure out where their number is and give you a clear understanding of where they stand. Some people may react strangely to this, but don't be intimidated. Make sure to have done proper research and analysis before offering up the price. It's important that your price range is reasonable for all parties or you may scare them away for good or offer them a price that would be a loss for you.

Another option you can try out is the "off the record" approach. There is a power with words which you should learn to utilize. Certain words can make people feel at ease while some can rile them up. Yes, you are not a journalist, but you can still use this phrase to your advantage. When people hear "off the record," it gives them the chance to loosen up. Just like earlier, you will say, "Off the record, can you share with me, in round numbers, how much you find acceptable?" By using the term " share" the prospect will feel a sense of belonging and a willingness to negotiate. Off the record and round numbers are key phrases here. Sharing is also a keyword. At this stage, it is also advisable to find out any factors that may affect their pricing and ability to make payments. Such details will help both parties reach an agreement and smoothen out details of the sale.

Price is an important factor affecting the completion of the entire sale. To be honest, if the price is right, the deal is closer to being done and vice versa.

CHAPTER 6

Uncover Timeframe

The timing for a sale is also equally important. How soon can the prospect get the deal over the line? How quickly do they want to make use of your service and enjoy the value that you are offering? When dealing with this aspect, the key is to not be direct. When prospects are directly asked about timing in relation to a deal, their natural instinct is to "protect their cards" by being dishonest. If you get lied to, it could change the entire scenario and make things even more difficult.

Due to this, the situation becomes quite dicey and could easily head in directions which you don't want it to. So, what do you do? The tactic you employ is to assume poorly. When you are speaking to the prospect, assume a very long timeframe—they will correct you. You would want to go long and assume they have all the time in the world. You could suggest a time of the year which is six to twelve months away. If they want something sooner, they will be the one doing the convincing, and you can finally settle on something that works for everybody. In a way, they are requesting that you close the sale faster than you normally would. This is positive for you as they will need to make a concession for that.

There are some customers who are unsure of how to handle timing. These people usually find it difficult to come to a conclusion about a suitable time. They would go on and on about why a particular timeframe is not favorable. Handling such people can quickly become frustrating. You can break them out of the loop of uncertainty by sharing a testimonial of a client who was quite similar to them and how you handled the whole issue on timing. By doing this, you let them trust in you and believe your professional ideas.

Don't ever be in a hurry to beat personal deadlines and push your prospect into a hurried decision. When you pressure prospects, they become tense and are likely to act. Things could quickly become unfavorable for you. You would never want a scenario where a client backs out of a sale because they feel it won't work out well for them. Remember that you are selling value. This means that you should be able to work with them and cooperate to get things concluded. Do not agree to terrible timing in the name of managing the prospect. Too much time can be dangerous too because they could change their decision before final negotiations are put to bed.

When would they like to have you serve them? If you have done a good job in selling value, they should be eager to work with you and get things over the line. This stage of the process hinges on how well you have directed the conversation in the earlier chapters. You may not get everything at once, but you have to put in the best effort.

CHAPTER 7

Uncover the Decision-Making Process

Can you think of any other industry that uses the word *decision* besides sales? The answer is likely no. There's something about the word that trips people up, whether it be car sales, house sales, insurance sales, etc. So far, you're doing well with your prospect. You've established rules, gone through the pain steps, and bonded with the client over great conversation—that is, until you say the word *decision*, and the whole car stops.

For whatever reason, some words have certain connotations. For example, I was doing a presentation online with some coworkers who were advertising it as a webinar. I said, "Guys, you cannot use the term webinar, because people will immediately think you're selling them something. Do not call it a *webinar*." Like webinar, decision is one of those words that you should remove from your sales lexicon.

Finding the Decision Makers

Without using the word decision, how do you find out who the decision maker is?

First, never ask "Who are the decision makers?" or "Will all the decision makers be present?" Likely, the husband puffs out his chest and says that he makes all the decisions; but this is rarely the case. For example, I'll often meet with the husband prior to meeting the wife and the conversation goes very well, so far. However, the self-proclaimed decision maker then goes to his wife, eyes downcast, and says what the offer is and tells her about my conversation with him. It turns out that the purpose of the "decision maker" was to gather information, not make a decision.

If you ask who the decision maker is and the husband or wife says, "I am," it's not the end of the world: you can still reply,

"You mean, you never get any help? You didn't run the sale by a family member, your accountant, or an attorney?" Well, yeah, the decision maker probably did talk to someone else before making a decision. And now you know who else is involved but not present in the sale.

Here are my go-to questions and statements for finding other decision makers or stakeholders:

Who else has input on this matter?

Who else will be impacted by this?

I assume nobody has veto power.

The aim of these three questions isn't to find out the ultimate, signing-the-contract decision makers, but to discover those who can talk the prospect out of making a decision. Once you find out who these people are, don't address them adversarially, saying why the prospect shouldn't listen to that person who could influence the sale. Ask if you can speak with them to answer any questions or concerns. For example, a prospect says that he will talk to his daughter before going through with the sale. This is your opportunity to ask the prospect if there's a time you can talk to the daughter, or all three talk together, when you can explain the process to her and address all her concerns. Now, by welcoming her and making her feel comfortable, the daughter will be on your side.

Now that we know how to find the decision makers, the next problem we must contend with is confirming terms.

CHAPTER 8

Confirming Terms

At this point, the sale is nearing the end—be sure to *not* introduce any new information from this point onward. If the prospect didn't bring it up before, you don't talk about it now. Countless sales have been ruined because I've brought up something that served only to confuse the ready prospect. That's a terrible waste when you consider the fact that their concerns were already satisfied prior to me bringing up more features and benefits. Remember, a confused mind does nothing.

Next, you should review the established rules. It's going to be a yes or a no, and anything besides a yes is a no. Remind the prospect of their previous agreements so that nothing changes in those terms going forward.

Review the prospect's pain. By bringing up each pain, the prospect is going to feel again why they're motivated to work with you. With this step, you're thinking "pain and feeling, pain and feeling," making that painful feeling fresh in the prospect's mind.

Review the number the prospect chose for the price, reminding the prospect that if they're not comfortable with the number, then we need to go back and fix it.

Also, review all the people who have input on the prospect's final decision. Is there anyone else that I don't know about? And if the prospect talks about someone new who could veto the whole sale, again ask if you can speak with them or you can all get together to answer any questions.

Finally, you've reached the natural conclusion close. It's as simple as five words: Do you want my help?

Objection Annihilator

Assuming you did everything right, you should never again hear the words, "I need to think about it." From time to time, though, you'll still get the thinking stall. When a prospect says that they need to think about it, ask them what about the sale do they need to think about:

You: "John , I'm a bit confused. In the beginning, we established that we were going to work together or not work together. Either way was fine. But you wouldn't tell me that you have to think about it. So I have to ask you, is it the price?"

Prospect: "No, no, no, it's not the price."

You: "Is it the process?"

Prospect: "Oh, no, no, it's not the process."

You, with a sad puppy face: "I get it . . . I understand . . . It's me."

Prospect: "No, no, no, it's not you! It's . . ."

And then they will tell you what it really is. When you assume poorly—in this case, stating that you're the mislabeled problem—the prospect will rush to correct you. And, because you feel bad about the issue being your fault, they'll naturally want to rescue you from your mistaken conclusion. Now they'll tell you what the problem really is.

CHAPTER 9

Prevent Remorse

We all know about buyer's remorse: making an emotional decision that's not necessarily a good financial decision—like going on vacation, getting overexcited, and buying a time share. Buyer's remorse can cause a sale to fall apart if remorse shows itself to the prospect before the sale is finalized. Until the money from a sale is in your bank account, you must work to keep the prospect engaged in the sale, even after the contract has been signed.

Causes of Buyer's Remorse

In my early days when a contract was signed, I'd shake the prospect's hand and take off, celebrating the sale. However, as we know, there's still a chance that the sale doesn't close. And until the money is in your bank account, the sale isn't over, and you can't celebrate.

If you don't address outside influences affecting the prospect, then you risk the sale falling through. Things that can torpedo a sale can include the prospect's family disrupting the sale and prospect's backing out and "going dark" right before the sale closed.

Your competition might be whispering sweet nothings into your prospect's ears while you're waiting for your sale to close as well. After all, they can reach your prospect through the same channels you did.

It's your job to prevent buyer's remorse. While waiting for your sale to close, you want to build a fence around the prospect so that the prospect has no room to regret their decision and back out of the sale.

Preventing Buyer's Remorse

There are three tactics that will prevent prospect's remorse taking away the sale: (1) reinforce the meaning of the sale, (2) give the option to cancel the sale early on, and (3) find out whether there's anyone who would object to the sale.

After signing the contract, turn the contract to face the prospect so that they can read it and ask, "What does this contract mean to you?" Sit there and allow them time to formulate an answer. It's likely that the prospect will respond it's a contract or just some papers.

Remind them that the contract solves a particular pain, such as paying off debts, allowing the prospect to move closer to grandchildren, giving the prospect freedom to travel, and so on. Previous chapters go into the importance of bringing up the prospect's pain, but after the prospect signs the contract there is one last opportunity to highlight the pain driving the sale.

Give them the option to back out of the sale by telling them that if they're uncomfortable for any reason at all—including with you—they should walk away from the deal and tear up the contract. It's better to confront this possible issue early on and actively, because the alternative is out of your control: the contract gets ripped up three weeks later without a word to you. Also, if you push someone to consider canceling the sale early on, he or she will be less likely to do so three weeks later after having affirmed commitment to the sale earlier.

You want to find out if there's anyone that would interject, stopping the sale from going through. What if the prospect's daughter doesn't want her parents to sell the house? Ask the prospect: What are you going to say to your daughter when she objects to the sale? The prospect will probably say that "it's our house, we own it, we can do what we want." This isn't a very convincing reason when the daughter starts poking at the terms of the deal. Have the prospect think: What obstacles will their daughter try to put in the way of the sale? You want to give the prospects reasons that address these obstacles if you want the sale to go through. The goal is to rehearse a scenario where the prospect is confronted by an objector and can persuade the objector, instead of being the one that's persuaded.

Now the prospects know what to say and think when confronted with objections, but make sure they know what to say if their contacted by your competition, who likely have professional sounding reasons for pulling the prospect away from your sale. Ask the prospects about what they will say to them. You want the prospect to be confident about saying, "Thank you, but we are committed to Steve, so we're good to go."

To prevent buyer's remorse, you must supply the prospect with reasons for still going through with the sale once that emotional high from signing the contract dissipates several days later. And the methods above cover the possible—and probable—scenarios where you can lose a prospect to influences outside of your control. But preemptively preparing the prospect against those influences will ensure the prospect doesn't go dark after the contract has been signed.

CHAPTER 10

Scorch the Earth

Let's have a brief history lesson and see what we learn from it. I can't remember where I read it. But the stories were about landmines.

If you are familiar with our business and our policy, then you understand that if we're not getting the contract, nobody's getting the contract. What do we do? We plant landmines under the welcome mat, under the sofa cushions, and in the kitchen cabinets. Why do we refer to this as a company policy?

This scorched earth practice has existed for thousands of years. It's a practice where warring parties destroy everything in their path when retreating. To deter enemy pursuit, they keep landmines in the ground. The most recent example of this was between

Germany and Russia during World War II. And they actually scorched the earth against each other. So, they would go and invade a certain part of each other's territory, and once they got past the borders, if they had to retreat, they would burn every village on the way out.

That's our corporate policy. And it's a very terrible experience. I mean, lots of casualties, but this is what we applied in our business in Phoenix. So, we named it the "Scorched Earth Policy."

In order to deliver an effective scorched earth policy, you'll need to come up with two or three unique selling propositions. If you get to a point in the meeting, and you see you're not getting the sale, you can adjust your position.

You will tell them that you are not able to help them. At this point, you will not be doing business together. And you ask them to write down a few things to prevent the prospect from doing business with your competition by asking them to write down your unique selling propositions (USP). And share with them, no matter what you do, be sure that the person they interview after you is able to deliver on your USPs. Because if they can't, that may be cause for concern.

When they ask the next vendor about your USPs, the next vendor may become flustered or frustrated. It's at this time that they will come back to you to work with you.

And so this can bring us back into the buyer world again, right? So, we practiced this earlier. Let me make sure that you're protected. You know, there's a lot of investors out there. I want to make sure that you learn to work right. If they talk to another vendor, then they may come back to you.

CHAPTER 11

Cold Calling Principles

Getting new customers for your sales company can be tough and expensive. There are some new companies who have it tougher than others, such as financial services and telecommunications companies. Every sales company is always concerned with bringing more people into the sales force. Many companies have adopted cold calling as a tactic to grow their customers.

A lot has been said about cold calling in the past, and it is not as complicated as it sounds. All you would need would be a phone, an email account, a social media account, and access to the customer. Take note that a cold call isn't just about calling.

The cold call also describes all form of cold contact which can be used to categorize a scenario when the person you are calling does not know who you are and what you want. It is a type of blind advertising where you try to attract the attention of a new customer within a few seconds. Cold calling includes cold emailing, phone calls, door-to-door sales, social media messages, and so on. In this chapter, we'll be taking a look at phone calls as examples, but you can apply the same principles to other media. The principles of a good cold call are universal and can surely produce good results.

During a cold call, you need to attract the attention of your prospect within the first few seconds of the call. To achieve desired results, you need to pay attention to the steps of a cold call. Without hitting these steps, your call will become flat.

Before you begin the call, be organized and make sure that you note a few things before you get started. Now, let's look at how you'll handle your cold calls:

1. Introduce yourself and gain attention

The first few seconds of your call are vital to how you create your impression. Your introduction has to be solid or you'll lose the rest of the call. As soon as they pick up, talk to them like they're your friend:

"Hey Sam!"

When you talk to them like you're their friend, you'll instantly gain their attention. You want to interrupt their pattern. The effect you're looking for is what you experienced the last time you were at a mall or supermarket and somebody you didn't recognize walked up and said hi to you by your first name. You were startled. That's your goal.

2. Tell them it's a bad time

Amateur salespeople ask, "Is now a good time?" Seasoned salespeople ask, "Is now a bad time?"

We outright tell prospects that it's a bad time, and they will tell us whether it is or not. It would sound like this: "It's Steve. Probably caught you at a bad time . . ."

3. What's this about?

At this time, you can describe some of the biggest challenges your clients face. Then tell them that those challenges probably don't apply in their situation.

"I've been working with clients that are frustrated about [common problem 1], disappointed about [common problem 2], or are overall tired about [common problem 3]. I don't suppose any of those apply to you . . ."

4. Actually, I've been dealing with [one of the common problems]

The rest of the time will be spent investigating their situation to find out whether we would be a good fit to schedule an appointment. The goal here is to increase the number of face-to-face appointments to increase your number of sales.

CHAPTER 12

Using Stories to Sell

In this chapter, we're going to talk about using a story to sell. Well, you guys may be using this already, and you don't realize it. And there is an old school methodology of studying sales. I've been studying sales since I got in the business back in 2007. This is the old school methodology. And there's nothing wrong with this methodology. It is actually is a very effective methodology. The only problem with it is that everybody knows it.

Feel. Felt. Found.

I understand how you feel. Other people have felt the same way. And when they found out . . .

If you're talking to someone in customer service, there are a few things you're going to hear a lot. I understand. How many times have you wanted to throw your phone at the wall because the guy says, "Oh, I understand exactly what you're saying," when they had no idea what you were saying?

Now, let's look at the third-party story. What are the benefits of using a third-party story? We want to convey that we understand their situation. Remember, we want the customer to feel understood. The second reason why we use a third-party story is that we're not in the crossfire. If you use a first-person story, you are talking about *I* and *we*. You don't want to talk about yourself.

We don't want to use a second-party story because second party stories talk about you and that's very accusatory. We could talk about your problems. We could talk about this and that, but we can't use you in this situation. So, what we're doing is using a third-party story. They can't cross-examine a third-party person.

The great thing about using a third-party story is that it fires up their brains the way that it's meant to be fired. So, if they're more audio-based when communicating, the audio section of their brain fires. If they're visual, the brain fires with the visual section.

The right sections are firing because they're putting themselves in that position when you use a third-party story. And last of all, we understand where they're standing. We know where they stand at the end of the third-party story. So what was the key? The third-party story is usually solid.

Describe somebody like your prospect. Okay. Remember when we're selling, they're the hero of the story. It's never about you. When we talk about features and benefits, you're the hero of the day that doesn't work when we're talking about them, they're the hero, they're in the hero's journey. That's when we can communicate. And that's how we can work together.

Let's describe for the prospects somebody like them. Describe somebody like them and describe the problem that they're having. For example, foreclosure was coming up and they wanted to move into an apartment. You just described the problem that's just like the problem with the person you're having at your face with. And then describe the consequence, consequences of that pain. You know, they're frustrated they're going through foreclosure, and then you identify the solution. That's the next part. But these are the keys. Don't bring in some irrelevant story. Don't talk about your weekend.

Talk about a story that applies very well to this specific situation. And if you can't come up with one, then what you want to do is that every time you have an objection, write down the objection you can't overcome. When you leave right before you've been driven away from your appointment, just write it down and think about one question you might have wanted to ask him or a third-party story that might've solved this problem. So I'll give you one story.

We have a lot of borrowers that come in and they want to use Wells Fargo, Bank of America, or Chase. Everyone wants to use the big banks. That's just how it works. Or they want to use an out-of-state bank because it's got the lowest interest rate.

Because they found some really low-interest rate on bank rate. And we always explain to them why they should not go with the lowest interest rate.

We've had a lot of clients that have gone through with the lowest interest rates. What happened was that during the transaction, it became more and more stressful because the big box bank doesn't actually care whether this loan closes or not. They just want to make sure that they have your money: that's really their priority. So, what ends up happening is we're going to be under a contract and you might be at risk of losing your earnest money because you couldn't close on time. So, that's using a third-party story that applies to that specific person.

I'll give you another example. You know, we got the election coming up. If someone asked you, Hey, are you voting for Biden or Trump? You might feel like you want to answer that question. But if you're talking to a prospect, you must never answer that question. So what do you say? You know, I was talking to my friends when we were having drinks last weekend and I was talking to the husband and he's a gung ho Trump supporter. I mean, he's really passionate about Make America Great Again. But the wife, she really loves what Biden has to say. Which do you think is right?

And then they'll tell you who they like. And now you can adjust accordingly. Remember you're not there to make friends, you're there to solve problems. Another way is by looking at a car example. I had a friend that just bought a new car, but because of their credit, and their impatience, they went bought the car and had lots of lenders. I know they're paying 13 percent. Do you think they made the right move?

ABOUT THE AUTHOR

Steve Trang trains some of the top real estate investors in the country on how to sell effectively.

Steve's legacy will be to create one hundred millionaires. One of his favorite quotes is from the great Zig Ziglar: "You can have everything in life you want, if you will just help enough other people get what they want."

He heard this quote when he first got into real estate, and it has stuck with him throughout his entire career. In fact, it's essentially one of the core values Steve lives by.

Since starting the brokerage in 2013, Stunning Homes Realty has over a hundred agents. In the Greater Phoenix area,

Stunning Homes Realty has almost 1 percent market share.

To get access to some of our free resources, please visit

www.activelistening20.com.